Criminal

Investigative

Policy &

Oversight

Evaluation of
Military Criminal Investigative Organizations'
Policies, Practices, and Procedures for
Investigations Involving Child Sexual Abuse

Report Number **CIPO2002S001**   January 11, 2002

Office of the Inspector General
Department of Defense

Additional Copies

To obtain additional copies of this evaluation report, visit the Inspector General, DoD, home page at http://www.dodig.osd.mil/dcis/cipo/evals.htm, or contact Mr. John Perryman, Project Manager, at (703) 604-8765 (DSN 664-8765).

Suggestions for Future Evaluations

To suggest ideas for or to request future evaluations, contact the Audit Followup and Technical Support Directorate at (703) 604-8940 (DSN 664-8940) or fax (703) 604-8932. Ideas and requests can also be mailed to:

OAIG-AUD (ATTN: AFTS Audit Suggestions)
Inspector General, Department of Defense
400 Army Navy Drive (Room 801)
Arlington, VA 22202-4704

Defense Hotline

To report fraud, waste, or abuse, contact the Defense Hotline by calling (800) 424-9098; by sending an electronic message to Hotline@dodig.osd.mil; or by writing to the Defense Hotline, The Pentagon, Washington, D.C. 20301-1900. The identity of each writer and caller is fully protected.

Acronyms

AFCCP	Armed Forces Center for Child Protection
AFOSI	Air Force Office of Special Investigations
APSAC	American Professional Society on the Abuse of Children
ASD(FMP)	Assistant Secretary of Defense (Force Management Policy)
CAPIT	Child Abuse Prevention and Investigative Techniques
CRC	Case Review Committee
DoD	Department of Defense
DoDD	Department of Defense Directive
DoDI	Department of Defense Instruction
FACAT	Family Advocacy Command Assistance Team
FAST	Family Advocacy Staff Training
FASTA	Family Advocacy Staff Training Advanced
IG, DoD	Inspector General, Department of Defense
MCIO	Military Criminal Investigative Organization
NAPA	National Academy of Public Administration
NCANDS	National Child Abuse and Neglect Data System
NCIS	Naval Criminal Investigative Service
RFC	Regional Forensic Science Consultant
SAC	Special Agent In Charge
SECNAV	Secretary of the Navy
USACIDC	U. S. Army Criminal Investigation Command
USD(P&R)	Under Secretary of Defense (Personnel and Readiness)

INSPECTOR GENERAL
DEPARTMENT OF DEFENSE
400 ARMY NAVY DRIVE
ARLINGTON, VIRGINIA 22202-4704

JAN 1 1 2002

MEMORANDUM FOR UNDER SECRETARY OF DEFENSE FOR PERSONNEL
READINESS
ASSISTANT SECRETARY OF THE ARMY (MANPOWER
AND RESERVE AFFAIRS)
ASSISTANT SECRETARY OF THE NAVY (MANPOWER
AND RESERVE AFFAIRS)
INSPECTOR GENERAL OF THE AIR FORCE

SUBJECT: Evaluation of Military Criminal Investigative Organizations' Policies,
Practices, and Procedures for Investigations Involving Child Sexual Abuse
(Report Number CIPO2002S001)

This report is provided for your review and comment. Your comments on the
draft report were considered in preparing the final report and are included in the final
report as Appendix H. Our responses to your comments are also discussed.

DoD Directive 7650.3 requires that all recommendations be resolved promptly.
We request your comments on the final report not later than February 28, 2002. We also
request your prompt action on our recommendations. Send your comments to the Office
of the Deputy Assistant Inspector General for Criminal Investigative Policy and
Oversight, 400 Army Navy Drive, Room 944, Arlington, Virginia, 22202-4704. Should
you have any questions, please contact Mr. John Perryman, Project Manager, at
(703) 604-8765 (DSN 664-8765) or jperryman@dodig.osd.mil.

We appreciate the courtesies extended to our evaluation staff throughout this
evaluation. The evaluation team members are listed inside the back cover. See
Appendix G for the report distribution.

Charles W. Beardall
Deputy Assistant Inspector General
Criminal Investigative Policy and Oversight

cc:
Commander, United States Army Criminal Investigation Command
Director, Naval Criminal Investigative Service
Commander, Air Force Office of Special Investigations
Commandant, U.S. Army Military Police School

TABLE OF CONTENTS

Executive Summary i

Part I - Background 1
    Evaluation Objectives, Scope, and Methodology 3

Part II - Evaluation Results 6
    A. Child Sexual Abuse in the Military 6
          National Versus Military Rates 6
          MCIO Work Time Devoted to Child Sexual Abuse Investigations 7
    B. Use of DoD Multidisciplinary Teams 8
          Policy 8
          Training 9
          Response to Allegations 9
          Team Member Coordination 10
        Management Comments and Our Evaluation 11
        Recommendation 13
    C. Interviewing Child Sexual Abuse Victims 13
          Use of Video to Record Victim Interviews 15
          Use of Anatomically Detailed Dolls in Victim Interviews 15
          Recent Training Enhancements 16
        Management Comments and Our Evaluation 17
        Recommendations 18
    D. Medical Examinations of Victims 19
    E. Interviewing Suspects in Child Sexual Abuse Investigations 20
    F. MCIO Support Resources 20
          Armed Forces Center for Child Protection 20
          Internal Support Resources 21
        Recommendations 22

Appendix A - Summary of NAPA Recommendations

Appendix B - Organizations with Effective Practices for Child Sexual Abuse
               Investigations

Appendix C - Survey of Law Enforcement Approaches to Investigating Allegations of
               Child Sexual Abuse (Concept Validation)

Appendix D - Summary Results from Statistical Random Sample

Appendix E - Policy, Regulation, or Program Guidance Addressing Challenges Unique
               to Child Sexual Abuse Investigations

Appendix F - Training that Addresses Challenges Unique to Child Sexual Abuse
               Investigations

Appendix G - Report Distribution

Appendix H - Management Comments

MILITARY CRIMINAL INVESTIGATIVE ORGANIZATIONS' POLICIES, PRACTICES, AND PROCEDURES FOR INVESTIGATING CHILD SEXUAL ABUSE

Executive Summary

Introduction. In January 2000, following a report by the National Academy of Public Administration (NAPA), the Deputy Secretary of Defense directed the Under Secretary of Defense for Personnel and Readiness (USD(P&R)), in cooperation with the Inspector General, Department of Defense, to review supporting roles and investigative functions in military child sexual abuse cases. The goal was to ensure an integrated approach to resourcing sexual misconduct investigations, particularly those involving child victims.[1] This evaluation responds to the Deputy Secretary's request as it concerns the military criminal investigative organizations (MCIOs).

Objectives. In researching professional literature and best practices, we identified four primary challenge areas unique to child sexual abuse investigations:

- They require a multidisciplinary approach, including activity coordination and information sharing among medical, social service, legal, and law enforcement communities.

- Criminal investigators require specialized training and knowledge to conduct effective victim interviews.

- Specialized medical examinations may be critically important to the investigation.

- Special considerations are involved in conducting suspect interviews.

Our primary objective was to determine whether DoD policy and training programs adequately addressed these unique challenges.

Results. Rates of child sexual abuse in the military are significantly lower than in the United States generally, and DoD policy and training appear adequate to address the primary challenges unique to child sexual abuse investigations. DoD, for example, requires the use of multidisciplinary teams that include law enforcement, medical, social services, and other professions in resolving child sexual abuse allegations. DoD

---

[1] Deputy Secretary of Defense Memorandum dated January 24, 2000, "SUBJECT: Implementation of the Recommendations of the National Academy of Public Administration."

policy prescribes team structure, participation, and responsibilities, and DoD trains investigators and other involved professionals based on the policy. Furthermore, the MCIOs recognize the special knowledge needed to interview child sexual abuse victims, and the MCIOs train their agents to ensure they have this knowledge.

We found that DoD has increased its emphasis on child sexual abuse investigations in the last few years, and this emphasis may not yet be fully reflected in the investigations we reviewed. Specifically, for investigations involving younger children (under 12 years old) completed during 1997 through 1999, MCIO investigative case files show coordination with social services personnel in 83 percent of the cases, coordination with medical personnel in 70 percent of the cases, and coordination with legal personnel in 67 percent of the cases. Similarly, the files show that MCIO agents interviewed about 49 percent of the victims under the age of 12, but in only 56 percent of those cases were the agents specially trained to interview child victims. The Army rate for use of specially trained agents was only 25 percent. We also identified segments of both Army and Navy training that lacked instructor guides and lesson plans with learning objectives that would ensure consistency in instruction and conformance with policy. Further, MCIO policies for using anatomically detailed dolls in child interviews are not fully consistent, although MCIO investigators rarely use that interview technique. The U.S. Army Criminal Investigation Command (USACIDC) and the Naval Criminal Investigative Service (NCIS) allow their agents to use anatomically detailed dolls if they have been trained in their usage. Air Force Office of Special Investigations (AFOSI) written policy allows agents to use *regular* dolls; it is silent on using anatomically detailed dolls, but agents are instructed not to use anatomically detailed dolls. The policy and training should complement each other.

In addition, DoD has special resources to support child sexual abuse investigations. In 1997, for example, the National Naval Medical Center established the Armed Forces Center for Child Protection (AFCCP) to provide consultative services for all DoD agencies needing objective medical expertise in suspected child maltreatment cases. MCIO program managers and child abuse specialists praise the AFCCP support they receive and regard it as indispensable to their missions. However, AFCCP has very limited funding that may prevent needed equipment acquisition and service expansion. See Part II of the report for details on the evaluation's findings.

Summary of Recommendations. We recommend that

- the MCIOs, during appropriate inspection, staff assistance, or oversight visits to field locations, verify that their criminal investigators involved in child sexual abuse investigations are participating in multidisciplinary teams, coordinating overall investigative activities, and sharing information throughout the investigations;

- USACIDC, through its Sex Crimes and Child Abuse Monitorship Program, give special emphasis to ensuring that only agents trained in interviewing children interview child sexual abuse victims;

- the U.S Army Military Police School block of instruction dealing with child interviews in the Child Abuse Prevention and Investigative Techniques course include a lesson plan with learning objectives and instructor guide to ensure consistency in instruction and conformance with Army policy;

- NCIS develop coordinated lesson plans with learning objectives and instructor guides to ensure consistency in training and conformance with NCIS policy;

- AFOSI written policy and training on the use of anatomically detailed dolls be consistent; and

- the USD (P&R) review the resources of the AFCCP and determine whether they should be enhanced.

Management Comments. On June 21, 2001, we issued this report in draft form for management comments. Between August 20 and December 20, 2001, we received comments from USD(P&R) and each of the Military Departments. Generally, they all concurred with the report. In response to our recommendations, USD(P&R) is increasing AFCCP funding; Navy developed lesson plans to enhance its training; and Air Force is reviewing its policy and will make changes in accordance with current research findings on using anatomically correct dolls. Although concurring with our report overall, the Army pointed out an apparent inconsistency in our statistics regarding the number of children under age 12 years included in our sample cases. We have amended the final report to overcome the apparent inconsistency. In addition, according to the Army, we did not address incident reporting timeliness in showing medical coordination rates in the draft report (Part II, Tables 3 and 4). The Army pointed out that, if an incident is not reported to investigators on a timely basis, medical evidence may be lost and a subsequent invasive medical examination might further traumatize the victim. We agree, and have amended language in the final report accordingly. The Army also requested that we amend the report in several areas based on its subsequent review of our sample cases. For the reasons described in the report body, we did not make additional amendments to the report based on the Army request. The management comments are addressed in detail in Part II of the report and are reproduced as Appendix H.

MILITARY CRIMINAL INVESTIGATIVE ORGANIZATIONS' POLICIES, PRACTICES, AND PROCEDURES FOR INVESTIGATING CHILD SEXUAL ABUSE

Part I - Background

In June 1999, the National Academy of Public Administration (NAPA) published a report for Congress pursuant to section 1072 of the National Defense Authorization Act for Fiscal Year 1998. In that report, *Adapting Military Sex Crime Investigations to Changing Times*, NAPA stated:

> Sex crimes are very personal violations that require a heightened degree of investigative skill and professionalism. Regardless of whether they occur in civilian or military life, investigators must consider the traumatic circumstances surrounding these crimes, and interact with victims who can be fearful, apprehensive, and uncertain.

> When the victims of sex crimes are children, the challenges for investigators are even greater. Interviewing children presents a formidable task. Investigators must determine the extent to which children can interpret questions, and they must understand that children are particularly susceptible to suggestive comments. Moreover, investigators must be skilled to deal with parents who do not always lend full-fledged support to investigators, especially if they are suspected of the crime. They must also maintain their objectivity in highly charged situations. Although the "sexual misconduct" category encompasses a wide range of sex crimes, child sexual abuse clearly is one area that is set apart by its very unique characteristics.[2]

NAPA summarized its position on child sexual abuse investigations as follows:

> Simply put, the investigation of child sexual crimes is different. Many investigative areas in the general crime arena require special talents and skills. Yet, the investigation of child sex crimes is especially unique. Interviewing children, young children in particular, requires special interest, talent and ability. Furthermore, dealing with parents, understanding the dynamics of child sexual offenders, and medical evidence are some of the other considerations which set this investigative area apart. To obtain quality child sex crimes investigators, agents need to be screened for these characteristics and then receive training to acquire the necessary skills.[3]

In DoD, the MCIOs[4] investigate serious crimes that involve DoD property,

---

[2] National Academy of Public Administration, *Adapting Military Sex Crime Investigations to Changing Times* (Washington: National Academy of Public Administration, 1999), 93.

[3] Ibid, 94.

[4] The MCIOs are the U.S. Army Criminal Investigation Command (USACIDC), the Naval Criminal Investigative Service (NCIS), and the Air Force Office of Special Investigations (AFOSI).

programs, or personnel. MCIO responsibility includes investigating allegations of child sexual abuse committed by Service members.[5] In addressing MCIO investigations of child sexual abuse, NAPA stated:

> Child sexual abuse occurs at a significant rate within the Armed Services. In 1997, the MCIOs initiated approximately nine hundred cases involving some type of child sexual abuse, or roughly one quarter of the total sex-related cases. That figure is not inconsistent with previous years. Simply put, investigating child sexual abuse in the military is not an anomalous undertaking. There is no reason to believe that its rate differs from society, taking into account the demographic differences.[6]

Overall, NAPA concluded:

> In most cases, DoD and the MCIOs have not put enough emphasis on investigating child sexual abuse. In addition, they have not done much to distinguish child sexual abuse investigations from other sex crime investigations. There are several problems, including inadequate policies and implementation, insufficient training, and the failure to assign personnel to ensure that MCIO units have well-qualified investigators for these cases.[7]

Although NAPA reported that it did not have sufficient time to give the investigation of child sexual abuse offenses the attention it deserved, its limited research suggested the following questions:

- Do DoD and the MCIOs recognize the unique challenges posed by child sexual abuse investigations? Do their policies, guidance, and training put enough emphasis and priority on such investigations?

- Are DoD and MCIO policies related to child sexual abuse investigations consistent, and are they uniformly implemented at the operational level?

- To what extent do MCIO assignment policies ensure that investigative units have agents with the interest, aptitude, and training needed to conduct child sexual abuse investigations?

- Is there an adequate support structure through which an agent can obtain resources during the course of a child sexual abuse investigation?

Although concluding that further study was needed and identifying substantial questions, NAPA recommended various actions related to child sexual abuse investigations. Those recommendations are summarized in Appendix A. DoD has not acted on those recommendations, pending the results of this evaluation.

As a result of the NAPA report, on January 24, 2000, the Deputy Secretary of

---

[5] Army Regulation 195-2, "Criminal Investigation Activities," October 30, 1995; Secretary of the Navy (SECNAV) Instruction 5520.3B, "Criminal and Security Investigations and Related Activities Within the Department of the Navy," January 4, 1993; and Air Force Instruction 71-101, volume 1, "Criminal Investigations," December 1, 1999.

[6] NAPA, op.cit., 94.

[7] Ibid.

Defense directed the USD(P&R), in cooperation with the IG, DoD, to review the supporting roles of personnel and programs under USD(P&R) aegis and MCIO investigative functions in child sexual abuse cases. The goal of the review was to ensure an integrated approach to resourcing sexual misconduct investigations, particularly those involving child victims.

This evaluation responds to the Deputy Secretary's request as it concerns the MCIOs. We announced this evaluation on June 27, 2000, and conducted our fieldwork from August through December 2000.

Evaluation Objectives, Scope, and Methodology

Our primary objective was to determine whether DoD policy and training programs adequately addressed the unique challenges of investigating child sexual abuse cases. In conducting research for this evaluation, we collected data on child sexual abuse in both the military and civilian sectors. We identified civilian and government organizations generally regarded by their peers as having effective practices in the investigation of child sexual abuse (see Appendix B). We interviewed officials from those organizations to identify areas they believed were unique to child sexual abuse investigations. In some cases, we reviewed their materials on training and operating practices so that we could identify noteworthy or unique investigative considerations used in their approaches to these investigations. To ensure that we understood the information they provided, we developed a survey instrument (see Appendix C) that personnel at each organization completed.

Our research disclosed that a variety of professions either are, or may become, involved when an allegation of child sexual abuse is investigated. In addition to the law enforcement officials who investigate the criminal aspect of the allegation, medical personnel, attorneys, social workers, clergy, and others may also become involved in their professional capacities. Unless their respective interests are incorporated into a cooperative process, their individual efforts taken in isolation can be counterproductive and may have an adverse impact on the potential for prosecution.

We also identified several aspects unique to child sexual abuse investigations that we believed merited closer examination. For example, as NAPA recognized, interviewing child sexual abuse victims, particularly young children, is different from interviewing adults. Interviewing younger victims requires special skills if law enforcement personnel are to collect all essential information while avoiding additional and unnecessary trauma to victims and their families. Furthermore, a competent physical examination of the victim may be vitally important to the investigation, and these examinations require health care practitioners who have specialized training and equipment. If law enforcement personnel do not recognize the importance of proper physical examinations of child victims of sexual abuse, they may not ensure that timely, complete, and appropriate examinations are conducted, and they may not ensure that the results of such examinations are presented and used properly in the ensuing investigation. Finally, although not dramatically different from other offender interviews, some special considerations are involved in interviewing suspects in child sexual abuse cases. In these cases, it is especially important to understand the offender's motivation. Based on our research, the following areas are the primary challenges unique to child sexual abuse cases:

- Child sexual abuse cases require a multidisciplinary approach, including coordination of the various aspects of the investigation and ensuring that information is shared among the participants.

- Criminal investigators require specialized training and knowledge of unique procedures that are essential for conducting effective victim interviews.

- Specialized medical examinations conducted by qualified caregivers may be important in supporting the investigation.

- Interviews of suspects require strategies that consider offenders' motivations and methods of operation for exploiting children.

After identifying these unique challenges of child sexual abuse investigations, we reviewed DoD, Military Department, and MCIO policy and training requirements to determine whether these challenges were adequately addressed. We also had each MCIO provide investigative data for sex crimes involving victims under age 18 years.[8] We specifically requested data on cases closed during calendar years 1997 through 1999. We limited our request to investigations in which the MCIO was the primary investigative agency.[9] In response to our request, the MCIOs submitted data on 1,725 cases (an average of 575 investigations per year). We then selected a random sample of these closed cases for detailed review and evaluation.[10] This resulted in the identification of 153 cases, 51 from each MCIO.

These 153 cases involved 155 individuals accused of sexual offenses against persons under age 18 years and 187 victims under age 18 years.[11] We visited the MCIOs and physically reviewed the case files to determine:

- the exact nature of the allegations that were investigated;

- the basic demographic data pertaining to the victims and subjects;[12]

- the prevalence of common investigative techniques;

---

[8] We used the following description of child sexual abuse in requesting MCIO case data: "Any form of legally prohibited sexual interaction with a minor under the age of 18. The term sex abuse includes forcible sexual assault, statutory rape, forcible or consensual oral or anal sodomy, forcible or consensual touching of the minor's genitals and buttocks (and if a female, her breasts), prostitution, and the videotaping and photographing of a minor in such sexual activity or in lewd and lascivious display of the genitals."

[9] This excluded cases in which the MCIOs merely assisted or monitored other law enforcement agency investigations.

[10] We used a stratified random sample design, with assistance from Inspector General statisticians. The results can be projected MCIO-wide at a 95 percent confidence level.

[11] Some investigations involved multiple offenders or multiple victims.

[12] In the criminal investigative community, the term "subject" or "investigative subject" is used to refer to a person suspected of having committed a crime.

- whether or not multidisciplinary teams were employed; and

- the qualifications of the MCIO agents who conducted child victim interviews.

We aggregated the 153 cases by the victim's age when the alleged abuse started in order to assess differences in the nature of the crimes investigated based upon the victims' age group.[13] Eighty-three cases (54 percent of the 153) and 102 victims (55 percent of the 187 victims) involved children under the age of 12. Appendix D, "Summary Results From Statistical Random Sample" summarizes the subject, victim, and abuse information from the 153 cases we evaluated.

---

[13] Age 12 years is typically regarded as the separation point between childhood and adolescence, and we adopted this as our threshold for distinguishing between age groups. Further, our assessments based on age are generally based on when the alleged abuse began. In some instances, however, such as in considering victim interview data, we based age considerations on when the victim was interviewed. See Table 5.

MILITARY CRIMINAL INVESTIGATIVE ORGANIZATIONS' POLICIES, PRACTICES, AND PROCEDURES FOR INVESTIGATING CHILD SEXUAL ABUSE

Part II - Evaluation Results

A.   Child Sexual Abuse in the Military

Although child sexual abuse does occur within the military community, the rate of victimization for military dependent children is significantly lower than the rate for the United States generally. The rate for the United States is 1.4 per thousand, and the rate for the military is 0.8 per thousand.

National Versus Military Rates

The U.S. Department of Health and Human Services compiles data from the States and reports information on child maltreatment in the National Child Abuse and Neglect Data System (NCANDS). For 1998, NCANDS categorized 99,278 reports of child sexual abuse as either substantiated or indicated, a rate of 1.4 per 1,000 children in the general population of the United States.[14] By comparison, as shown in Table 1, the rate of child sexual abuse in the Military Departments ranged from 0.3 to 1.1 per thousand military dependent children, and averaged 0.8 per thousand overall. Thus, the NCANDS-reported rate for the United States is higher than the average military rate.[15]

---

[14] U.S. Department of Health and Human Services, Administration on Children, Youth and Families, *Child Maltreatment 1998*: *Reports from the States to the National Child Abuse and Neglect Data Systems* (Washington DC: U.S. Government Printing Office, 2000), pages E-3 and E-11. NCANDS excludes data for the States of Maryland, Massachusetts, and North Dakota, which did not report sexual maltreatment information to NCANDS for 1998.

[15] We believe this comparison is reasonable and usable for all general purposes. NCANDS data are compiled from individual State reports and are based on individual State laws and definitions, including the age constituting a child for reporting purposes. Further, the States report "substantiated or indicated" abuses, again subject to individual State definitions.

Table 1. Rates of Child Sexual Abuse in the Military

Military Department	Dependent Children <u>Under Age 18 Years</u>*	Substantiated Child Sexual Abuse Reports**	Rate per 1,000
Army	436,809	420	1.0
Navy	319,315	356	1.1
Air Force	342,185	205	0.6
Marine Corps	102,376	31	0.3
Total	**1,200,685**	***1,012	**0.8**

* 1998 population data provided by Director, Family Advocacy Program, Military Community and Family Policy, Office of the Assistant Secretary of Defense (Force Management Policy).

** DoD Directive 6400.1, "Family Advocacy Program," enclosure 2, June 23, 1992, defines substantiated as "[a] case that has been investigated and the preponderance of available information <u>indicate</u> that abuse has occurred. This means that the information that supports the occurrence of abuse is of greater weight or more convincing than the information that indicates that abuse did not occur [emphasis added]." Each Military Department's Family Advocacy Program uses this definition in reporting substantiated cases, which should make their reports reasonably comparable with the NCANDS category of substantiated or indicated. The Military Department Family Advocacy Program Offices provided the reports used for this table.

*** These reports of abuse do not necessarily indicate a Service member victimized the child.

MCIO Work Time Devoted to Child Sexual Abuse Investigations

The MCIOs devote approximately 6 percent of their total work time to the investigation of allegations of child sexual abuse, as shown in Table 2.

Table 2. Percent of Total Work Time Devoted to Child Sexual Abuse Investigations*

MCIO	Calendar Year		Average
	1998	1999	
USACIDC	5.02	5.57	5.30
NCIS**	7.00	7.76	7.38
AFOSI**	8.00	4.00	6.00
Average***	6.67	5.78	6.23

* Prior to implementing a new computer system in 1997, AFOSI did not collect this type of data.

** Percent determinations exclude NCIS and AFOSI foreign counterintelligence work.

*** Simple average. The MCIOs reported their individual annual percentages, but not the hours used to calculate those percentages.

B.   Use of DoD Multidisciplinary Teams

DoD policies require multidisciplinary teams and information sharing in addressing child sexual abuse complaints. Additionally, these requirements are included routinely in training.

According to the U.S. Department of Justice, Office of Justice Programs, the most effective approach to child maltreatment cases is through the use of multidisciplinary teams that include police, social workers, physicians, attorneys, and other professionals. These multidisciplinary teams plan and coordinate the investigations, resolve internal differences, and determine the best way to meet the needs of the child while resolving the criminal allegation.[16] The use of multidisciplinary teams therefore augments and extends investigator qualifications and can effectively negate the deficit that accrues when the investigation is handled solely by an investigator (especially one who is inexperienced in child sexual abuse investigations).

Policy

DoD requires the use of multidisciplinary teams to resolve child sexual abuse allegations.[17] DoD policy (both DoD-wide and at the Military Department level) prescribes team structure, participation, and responsibilities of multidisciplinary teams. This policy is part of the DoD Family Advocacy Program, which the Office of Family Policy, Office of the Assistant Secretary of Defense (Force Management Policy) (ASD(FMP)), directs.[18] The multidisciplinary teams are commonly referred to as Case Review Committees (CRCs). A CRC is defined in DoD Directive 6400.1 as "a multidisciplinary team of designated individuals working at the installation level, tasked with the evaluation and determination of abuse and/or neglect cases and the development and coordination of treatment and disposition recommendations."

The Military Departments implement this policy either as part of their personnel function (Navy) or as a medical function (Army and Air Force). At the installation level, the variously named CRCs all require representatives of the medical, social services, legal, law enforcement, and investigative communities to share information they have on each child sexual abuse case. The alleged abuser's military unit is encouraged to participate and may attend the meetings. The CRC sends its recommendations to the subject's commander for action.

---

[16] U.S. Department of Justice, Office of Justice Programs Guide, "Law Enforcement Response to Child Abuse," May 1997.

[17] DoD Directive 6400.1, "Family Advocacy Program," June 23, 1992.

[18] The DoD Family Advocacy Program addresses family violence prevention, identification, evaluation, treatment, rehabilitation, follow up, and reporting. The program consists of coordinated efforts to prevent and intervene in cases of family distress, and to promote healthy family life.

Training

The Army offers specialized multidisciplinary training attended by other Services. As explained below, we were unable to adequately assess the Navy Family Advocacy training.

The Army also offers advanced training under Family Advocacy Staff Training Advanced (FASTA). FASTA training is actually a group of 1-week courses targeting a multidisciplinary audience and presents special family advocacy issues. Two of these courses were relevant to our evaluation.

- The multi-victim FASTA course is a 1-week course designed to develop interdisciplinary skills of CRC members, including law enforcement personnel and criminal investigators, in managing out-of-home allegations of child sexual abuse in DoD-sanctioned activities, such as child development centers. The course trains CRC members to use a systematic method to interview children in order to ensure validity. The course also teaches members how to organize and use community resources to manage incidents in which there may be multiple victims.

- The 1-week forensic child sexual abuse FASTA course develops the skills of clinicians, counselors, investigators, and medical professionals who are directly involved in handling child sexual abuse investigations. The training focuses on forensic interviews, treatment modalities, counseling the non-offending parent, and preparing the professional to advocate for the child in court.

The Army Family Advocacy Staff Training (FAST) course trains Army, Air Force, and Marine Corps military and civilian personnel. For 2 weeks, social workers, psychologists, military police, criminal investigators, lawyers, physicians, prevention specialists, victim advocates, nurses, and Family Advocacy Program managers are trained on the DoD Family Advocacy Program. FAST emphasizes the roles of the various disciplines and their productive interactions to intervene and manage domestic violence and child abuse, including child sexual abuse. FAST trained 1,175 students during FYs 1998 through 2000.

The Navy Family Advocacy Program has a 32 to 36 hour training course for military and civilian CRC members. According to the NCIS Child Sexual Abuse Program Manager (who teaches at the course), the course emphasizes understanding the roles and responsibilities of the various disciplines affecting the CRC team approach to resolving allegations of domestic violence and child abuse, including child sexual abuse. However, the program manager advised us that no lesson plans, syllabi, course outlines, or descriptions of the course existed. We, therefore, were unable to review the training in detail.

Response to Allegations

When an instance of child sexual abuse is alleged, DoD responds with specially trained and organized groups. The number of victims, the notoriety of the investigation, and the local availability of resources govern the size and scope of any given response to an allegation of child sexual abuse.

Within the Military Departments, the Family Advocacy Program (FAP) is the primary program for responding to child sexual abuse allegations. Under each FAP, the Military Departments created specialized structures for dealing with child sexual abuse. Army installations rely on CRCs, but have latitude to establish separate, specialized CRCs to respond to child sexual abuse allegations.[19] Navy installations use the Navy Regional Child Sexual Abuse Response Team.[20] Air Force installations use the Child Sexual Maltreatment Response Team.[21] In each case, the teams are multidisciplinary and include MCIO representatives.

Under FAP, upon a component request, ASD(FMP) launches a Family Advocacy Command Assistance Team (FACAT).[22] FACATs commonly include investigators and specialists in social services, pediatrics, psychology/psychiatry, law, family advocacy, childcare administration, and the education disciplines. The teams are normally deployed in response to allegations of multiple-victim child sexual abuse incidents arising in family childcare facilities, child developmental centers, youth programs, DoD schools, or other DoD-sanctioned activities. Teams consist of personnel in the Military Departments who have received special training sponsored by the ASD(FMP). FACAT team members are experienced in their professional capacities and train jointly on interactions among their respective specialties. FACAT training takes a full week and is generally given to 70 - 80 people every 3 to 4 years (the last time it was offered was in 1998). Most people who receive FACAT training are civil service employees who remain in their positions or who move to a similar position in a different Military Department. FACAT training focuses on understanding and exploiting the resources each specialty possesses to solve multiple-victim, out-of-home child sexual abuse allegations. From 1997 through 1999, FACATs deployed three times to help resolve possible child sexual abuse allegations involving a total of 148 children.

Appendixes E and F detail DoD policy and training, respectively, for responding to child sexual abuse allegations. DoD policy requires using multidisciplinary teams and the sharing of information in these types of cases. In addition, the response requirements are routinely trained.

Team Member Coordination

Multidisciplinary teams that conduct DoD child sexual abuse investigations are required to coordinate their activities and share information. In reviewing a random sample of closed cases at the respective MCIO headquarters, we noted each instance in which the files indicated that investigative activities were coordinated with legal, medical, or social services personnel. Tables 3 and 4 present our findings based on whether the victims were over or under 12 years of age.

---

[19] Army Regulation 608-18, "The Army Family Advocacy Program," September 1, 1995, paragraph 2-3.b.

[20] OPNAV Instruction 1752.2A, "Family Advocacy Program," July 17, 1996, paragraph 5.

[21] Air Force Instruction 40-301, "Family Advocacy," July 2, 1994, paragraphs 1.5 and 2.3.1.

[22] DoD Instruction 6400.3, "Family Advocacy Command Assistance Team," February 3, 1989.

Table 3. Coordination Reflected in Investigative Files
Victims Under Age 12 Years
(Percent of Total Victims Per Service)

MCIO	Type Organization Involved in MCIO Coordination		
	Legal	Social Services	Medical
USACIDC	77	73	45
NCIS	77	88	77
AFOSI	48	87	87

Table 4. Coordination Reflected in Investigative Files
Victims Age 12 Years and Over
(Percent of Total Victims Per Service)

MCIO	Type Organization Involved in MCIO Coordination		
	Legal	Social Services	Medical
USACIDC	61	31	22
NCIS	71	58	26
AFOSI	66	58	45

As can be seen in Tables 3 and 4, the review of MCIO investigative files disclosed substantial coordination with legal, medical, and social services, especially when the victims were younger. They did not, however, show coordination in all or virtually all such investigations, as would be expected based on DoD policy and training. On the other hand, these tables are based on data available in the MCIO case files maintained at headquarters, which may not include information on all actual coordination. USACIDC and NCIS agents do not send their entire criminal investigative files to headquarters for retention. Some documentation, such as agent's notes and case memorandums, is generally retained in local field office investigative files. Therefore, the actual rates of coordination may be higher than the levels shown in Tables 3 and 4. Nonetheless, to ensure full compliance with policy, the MCIOs should take steps to make certain that coordination and information sharing occurs routinely in *all* child sexual abuse investigations. This could be accomplished during recurring inspections, staff assistance visits, and internal oversight visits to MCIO field locations.

Management Comments and Our Evaluation

The Military Departments all concurred with our report. In its comments, however, the Army questioned the USACIDC statistics reported in Tables 3 and 4, indicating that they were not consistent with USACIDC findings in a subsequent re-evaluation of the sample cases. According to the Army comments, USACIDC completed legal coordination in all but one case in the sample and this case was referred to FBI for follow-on investigative work. Further, the Army indicated that the medical coordination percentages reported for USACIDC might not be accurate representations, since the report did not consider whether incidents were reported on a timely basis. According to the Army, if an incident is not reported timely, a subsequent invasive medical examination can further traumatize the victim. Therefore, the Army indicated that the report should be modified to reflect actual USACIDC legal coordination in the sample cases, as well as to reflect that medical coordination might not always be required or conducted if the incident is not reported in a timely manner.

We do not agree. The data that was reported represent the coordination reflected in the headquarters case files when we completed our fieldwork. In presenting this data, we specifically advised that the headquarters files, might not reflect the full coordination completed in Army and Navy cases. Furthermore, although we agree that untimely reporting of an incident could result in a lost opportunity to collect evidence through a medical examination, we do not present judgments on the need for specific forensic medical examinations. Tables 3 and 4 only display whether we saw indications that alleged child sexual abuse was coordinated with medical professionals.

Though not tied to a particular recommendation, the Army also questioned our statistical sampling methodology and suggested that it be refined in future studies. According to the Army, USACIDC accounted for 55 percent of the total investigations from which our sample was taken, with NCIS and AFOSI accounting for the remaining 45 percent. As a result, the Army indicated that a statistical sampling should have resulted in about twice as many USACIDC cases being reviewed, but each MCIO had about the same number of cases reviewed. Since USACIDC investigates about twice as many child assaults as the other MCIOs, the Army requested that we include an additional recommendation that USACIDC receive twice the number of training allocations as the other MCIOs.

We understand the Army's concern that its larger case proportion did not result in a larger sample proportion. However, the random sampling methodology that we applied was valid to the 95 percent confidence level and produced results that may be projected to the overall case universe with the same confidence level. Accordingly, there is no reason to adjust our sampling methodology for future studies. In addition, although OUSD(P&R) funded some Family Advocacy Program training prior to FY 1998, the Services now fund their own training. In fact, since FY 1998, the Army has continued to authorize and fund the FAST course and invites the other Services to purchase training slots for FAST. Accordingly, the Army establishes its own training allocations, and there is no reason for us to recommend that it be given additional allocations.

Recommendation

1. The Military Criminal Investigative Organizations, during recurring inspection, staff assistance, and oversight visits to field locations, verify that criminal investigators involved in child sexual abuse investigations are in all such cases participating in multidisciplinary teams, coordinating overall investigative activities, and sharing information throughout the investigations.

Management Comments: The Services all concurred with the recommendation. Air Force commented that its current Unit Compliance Inspection process (UCI) includes reviewing the detachment's closed investigative files for sufficiency and documentation and, in reviewing any child sexual abuse investigation, the inspectors verify that coordination was completed with a Forensic Science Consultant, as well as with medical and legal authorities. The comments are responsive to our recommendation.

C.   Interviewing Child Sexual Abuse Victims

According to the American Professional Society on the Abuse of Children (APSAC), at a minimum, investigators who interview children should have some familiarity with

- basic concepts of child development,
- communication abilities of children,
- dynamics of abuse and offenders,
- categories of questions necessary for a thorough investigation,
- legally acceptable child interview techniques, and
- the use of interview aids.[23]

The APSAC guidelines stress that this familiarity is especially important when investigators interview younger children.

For DoD, there are no specified training requirements for police officers or criminal investigators who interview child sexual abuse victims.[24] Nonetheless, Military Department and MCIO policies address the need for investigators who interview child sexual abuse victims to understand child development, the nature of the sex crime, and legally acceptable interview techniques,[25] as demonstrated in Appendix E. Each MCIO now familiarizes its agents with these aspects relevant to child interview issues during

---

[23] "APSAC Guidelines on Investigative Interviewing in Cases of Alleged Child Abuse," April 2000.

[24] FAP has education and licensure requirements for diagnostic assessment interviews when the sexual abuse victim is a child. These requirements are set forth in DoD Manual 6400.1-M, "Family Advocacy Program, Standards and Self-Assessment Tool," August 1992.

[25] MCIO efforts in this area expanded after NAPA began its evaluation in 1998. See Recent Training Enhancements on page 15 of this report.

their basic training for special agents. Furthermore, the MCIOs, through policy and practice, ensure that their agents have substantial access to specialized resources when conducting child sexual abuse investigations (see "MCIO Support Resources," page 20). Each MCIO also offers advanced, specialized training on interviewing child sexual abuse victims (see Appendix F). Overall, the MCIOs do not train apprentice agents to conduct specialized child forensic interviewing; however, we believe MCIO advanced training prepares agents adequately to conduct interviews in child sexual abuse cases.

We reviewed our sample of closed investigative cases to determine whether the MCIO agents who interviewed child victims had received specialized training. During the 3 years included in our review (1997-1999), 79 victims of child sexual abuse were under 12 years of age when first interviewed. Of these victims, an MCIO agent interviewed 39 (49 percent) of them.[26] The proportion of these 39 interviews that were conducted by agents who received specialized training is shown in Table 5.

Table 5. MCIO Victim Interviews
Conducted by Specially Trained Agents
(Victims Under Age 12 Years at Initial MCIO Interview)

MCIO	1997	1998	1999	Total	Percent
USACIDC					
Number of victims interviewed	3	6	7	16	
Specialized interviews*	0	3	1	4	25
NCIS					
Number of victims interviewed	3	2	2	7	
Specialized interviews*	2	2	2	6	86
AFOSI					
Number of victims interviewed	7	1	8	16	
Specialized interviews*	4	0	8	12	75
Total MCIOs					
Number of victims interviewed	13	9	17	39	
Specialized interviews	6	5	11	22	56

*A specially trained MCIO agent conducted interview.

As can be seen in Table 5, specially trained agents interviewed 22 of the 39 victims (56 percent). The relatively low overall percent of interviews conducted by specially trained agents is disproportionately influenced by the USACIDC totals, where specially trained agents conducted only 25 percent of the interviews. However, upon closer examination, we found that

- a social worker assisted 4 of the 12 USACIDC agents who interviewed without specialized training,

---

[26] A child protective service worker, local police detective, child interview specialist, or other professional normally interviewed victims who were old enough to interview and whom a MCIO agent did not interview.

- a social worker assisted the one NCIS agent who interviewed without specialized training, and

- a social worker assisted three of the four AFOSI agents who interviewed without specialized training.

It is unclear whether or not having a social worker present during these interviews adequately offset the agent's lack of specialized training. It is clear, however, that the MCIOs *have* increased their emphasis on child sexual abuse investigations and related training subsequent to the period covered in our case reviews (see Recent Training Enhancements, page 16). For example, subsequent to the child interviews in the cases we reviewed, 10 of the 12 USACIDC agents without specialized training who interviewed the children have been given the specialized training.

Use of Video to Record Victim Interviews

One area, that NAPA identified as clearly illustrating discrepancies and inconsistencies among MCIO child sexual abuse investigations, involved videotaping child interviews. When interviewing field agents, NAPA encountered a variety of personal preferences that ranged from videotapes helping "... minimize trauma suffered by child victims ..." to videotapes being "... hotly debated in courtrooms ..." and discouraged by prosecutors. We found that each MCIO has policy *allowing* video recordings, and each has training on properly using video-recording equipment. However, the MCIOs all require investigators to coordinate with the local staff judge advocate before videotaping an interview. Of the interviews of 39 younger children conducted by MCIO agents, 19 (49 percent) were videotaped. We think this coordinated approach, the previously mentioned current MCIO policies limiting the interviews of child sexual abuse victims to specially trained agents, and Recommendation 2 effectively address the NAPA concerns.

Use of Anatomically Detailed Dolls in Victim Interviews

Another area addressed in the NAPA report involved the use of anatomically detailed dolls during the course of child interviews. We found that MCIO investigators rarely used this interview technique. Of the 39 younger children interviewed by MCIO agents, only 2 (5 percent) involved the use of anatomically detailed dolls. USACIDC and NCIS allow their agents to use anatomically detailed dolls if the agents have been trained in their use.[27] AFOSI guidance allows agents to use *regular* dolls, but is silent on the issue of using anatomically detailed dolls. According to the AFOSI program manager (who is also the AFOSI Command Psychologist and the person who conducts all AFOSI training on interviewing child sexual abuse victims), she instructs AFOSI agents to *not* use anatomically detailed dolls. Instead, she trains them to use a drawing technique designed to be stimulus neutral, allowing children to express something that may be too difficult to verbalize. She stated that she believes anatomically detailed dolls are not a

---

[27] The outside organizations and agencies that we consulted during our evaluation all agreed that only agents trained to use anatomically detailed dolls should use them.

substantive benefit during interviews and can be distracting to the child because they "probably do not look like" any doll the child has seen. As a result, she says their appearance can be startling to a child.

As is apparent, MCIO policy on the use of anatomically detailed dolls is not consistent. This situation generally reflects the uncertainty that exists in the professional community. In *The Sexual Exploitation of Children, A Practical Guide to Assessment, Investigation, and Intervention,* the author points out that using anatomically detailed dolls in child interviews is controversial. He cites instances when a professional may be able to use the dolls effectively, but concludes that their use is not mandatory and that a "...child's own dolls often work as well, if not better, because the child will be more familiar with them and have little or no fear of using them."[28] Similarly, APSAC guidelines acknowledge concerns that the dolls may be suggestive, encourage false reports, or be traumatizing, but conclude that they may enhance an interview *when used by knowledgeable, experienced professionals.* Overall, APSAC concludes that additional research is needed in this area.[29] We agree. We also agree that this interview technique is controversial and that only well-trained and experienced personnel should attempt its application in child victim interviews. USACIDC and NCIS have clear policy regarding this technique. AFOSI does not have clear policy, but has operating practices that preclude using the interview technique. AFOSI should adopt specific policy and not rely on implementation of policy through training decisions. The MCIOs should stay abreast of research in this area to adapt their policies as appropriate.

Recent Training Enhancements

In recent years, the MCIOs have taken actions to enhance their agents' skills in conducting child abuse investigations. In 1999, the Commander, USACIDC, established child abuse investigations as a core competency. As a result, all USACIDC agents are required to attend the Army's Child Abuse Prevention and Investigative Techniques (CAPIT) course (referenced in Appendix F). By September 30, 2000, USACIDC had sent 58 percent of its agents to this training. By FY 2004, USACIDC expects 90 percent of its agents will have completed this training.

NCIS and AFOSI have begun using specialized child forensic interview training to enhance their agents' skills. The Navy Family Advocacy Program contracted with APSAC and began this type of training in 1999.[30] AFOSI developed its Advanced Field Agent's Course on Child Forensic Interviews (referenced in Appendix F) in 1998. NCIS is training approximately 25 agents per year, and AFOSI is training approximately 40 agents per year.

---

[28] Seth L. Goldstein, *The Sexual Exploitation of Children, A Practical Guide to Assessment, Investigation, and Intervention* (Boca Raton: CRC Press LLC, 1999), 270-271.

[29] American Professional Society on the Abuse of Children, *Practice Guidelines, Use of Anatomical Dolls in Child Sexual Abuse Assessments* (Chicago: American Professional Society on the Abuse of Children, 1995), 2-4.

[30] Future Navy Family Advocacy Program child interviewing courses will incorporate APSAC training components, but will be opened to competitive-bid contracting.

The Army, Navy, and Air Force training identified in Appendix F conforms in large measure to the APSAC guidelines for interviewing child victims. All MCIOs have policies or guidance stressing that only people trained to interview children should conduct these interviews. Our review of the policies, training, and investigative cases sustain the conclusion that the MCIOs understand the unique challenges involved in interviewing children and that they are making substantive, continuing efforts to improve their competence in this area.

Management Comments and Our Evaluation

The Military Departments all concurred. The Army, however, questioned the different numbers that we reported for victims under the age of 12 years involved in our analyses. As we pointed out in the draft report (see Footnote 13 in the final report), we generally based age assessments on when the alleged abuse began; however, those assessments involving interviews were based on victim age when the MCIO first interviewed the victim. To avoid further opportunity for confusion on this issue, we have clarified the information introducing Table 5, as well as the Table 5 heading, to make clear that the victims involved were those who were under age 12 years when first interviewed by the MCIO.

The Army also commented that we did not credit three 1997 Army interviews as being conducted by specially trained agents. This comment apparently derives from notations on a worksheet that we sent to the Army while it was evaluating the draft report. The Army requested a list of its specific cases that we reviewed where the victims were under age 12 years when interviewed. Our worksheet noted the agents who had attended FAST courses overall. One FAST course, however, did not include specialized child interview training. Three USACIDC agents who conducted child interviews in 1997 attended this course. We credited all MCIO agents, including USACIDC agents, with attending the FASTA courses that covered child interviewing (see Section B, Training).

In addition, the Army asserts that our inability to evaluate NCIS specialty training in as much detail as we were able to evaluate USACIDC specialty training should be noted specifically at Table 5. We do not agree. The fact that NCIS did not have lesson plans or instructor guides for specialized child interview and follow-on training, which required us to rely on presentation slides in reviewing this training, is already amply discussed in the report (see Appendix F, and Section F, MCIO Support Resources, Navy) and is the basis for a separate recommendation to NCIS (Recommendation 6).

Finally, the Army states that we did not evaluate individual USACIDC agent backgrounds, and some have received specialized training in child development and training in college courses, unit training, or local/regional discretionary training with other law enforcement agencies. In addition, the Army states that every USACIDC agent receives 12 hours of child interview specific training in the apprentice special agent course, and 480 USACIDC agents have received advanced specialty training since 1997. According to the Army, giving full credit for this training might well increase the training percentages. We agree. However, that was not the basis for our evaluation of MCIO training. Our evaluation focused on the training that best reflected the MCIO policies and procedures and, specifically, whether agents received specific, advanced training to equip them to deal with the unique challenges involved in interviewing child sexual abuse victims. As a result, we did not include basic agent training for any MCIO. Furthermore, to the extent that USACIDC agents have met advanced training requirements through previous college, unit, or local/regional training, we would expect to see records waiving specific individuals from requirements to attend advanced training by or for the MCIO. We did not see such records. During our evaluation, however, we did submit the names of the 16 USACIDC agents who interviewed victims under age 12 years to the FASTA course manager and the CAPIT course manager. These managers identified training these individuals had attended based on their records, and this information was taken into account in developing Table 5.

Recommendations

2. **We recommend that the U.S. Army Criminal Investigation Command, through its internal oversight program, give special emphasis to ensuring that agents who interview victims of child sexual abuse have been trained to interview children.[31]**

Management Comments. The Army concurred, but did not identify how it intends to give this special emphasis. In commenting on the final report, the Army should provide further detail, including the specific action(s) it will take and when it began or expects to begin taking the individual actions.

3. **We recommend that the U.S. Army Criminal Investigation Command adopt a lesson plan with learning objectives and instructor guide for its block of instruction dealing with child interviews in the Child Abuse Prevention and Investigative Techniques training program.**

Management Comment. The Army concurred, advising that U.S. Army Military Police School (USAMPS) lesson plans for child interviews are being converted into one lesson plan to be taught by USAMPS subject matter experts, and the new lesson plan incorporates all information identified in our evaluation. In commenting on the final report, the Army should provide estimated completion dates for the new lesson plan and for implementing the new plan in actual training.

4. **We recommend that because Air Force Office of Special Investigations instructs its agents to not use anatomically detailed dolls during the interview of children, such guidance should be incorporated in its written policy.**

Management Comments. The Air Force concurred, advising that AFOSI policy

---

[31] We expect that NCIS and AFOSI will continue at the high ratio of specially trained agents doing these types of interviews as established in the 1999 statistics we developed.

would be reviewed and changes *recommended* based on current research findings on using anatomically detailed dolls. Estimated completion date for the action was December 1, 2001. In commenting on the final report, Air Force should update this information, including an estimated completion date for implementing the revised policy.

D.   Medical Examinations of Victims

The Department of Justice points out that "[m]edical evidence can provide powerful and convincing corroboration to an allegation of sexual abuse."[32] Although it is clear that people who receive training in sexual abuse forensic examinations should be the ones to conduct such examinations, they are not always available. Dr. Barbara Craig, Armed Forces Center for Child Protection, National Naval Medical Center, Bethesda, Maryland, provided 1998 survey information revealing that 70 percent of the faculty and 63 percent of the residents in pediatric training programs thought they did *not* learn enough to perform child sexual abuse evaluations. Criminal investigators do not conduct those examinations, but we believe they should have some knowledge of the evidence that might be obtained from a forensic medical examination. The external agencies we contacted and the Department of Justice advised that criminal investigators should be familiar with the protocols that comprise a medical examination in sexual assault cases.[33]

Based on our case reviews, 48 victims under age 12 years (61 percent of the total) received medical examinations. We believe that less than half (46 percent) of those examinations had been conducted by medical personnel who were specifically trained in conducting sexual assault examinations.[34] In our view, these results validate the need to train MCIO agents on evidence that might be obtainable from a medical examination of a victim of child sexual abuse. Such training enhances their ability to advise medical personnel unfamiliar with the procedures.

As Appendix E and Appendix F indicate, the MCIOs have policies and training that address evidence obtainable from a medical examination. We note in particular that the Army's medical "Protocol For Child Abuse and Neglect" and the Army Installation Handbook, *Managing Out of Home Child Sexual Abuse Cases*, both used for training in the CAPIT course, include exceptionally good information on forensic medical examinations.

---

[32] U.S. Department of Justice, Office of Justice Programs Guide, "Criminal Investigation of Child Sexual Abuse," May 1997.

[33] U.S. Department of Justice, Office of Justice Programs Guide, "Criminal Investigation of Child Sexual Abuse," May 1997.

[34] Our conclusion in this respect is based on various factors. For example, if (a) a sexual assault center conducted the examination, (b) a child protective service referred the victim to the healthcare provider or clinic, or (c) detail in the medical exam report indicated a knowledge of forensic medical examinations, we counted the examination as having been conducted by medical personnel trained in sexual assault examinations.

E.   Interviewing Suspects in Child Sexual Abuse Investigations

The external agencies we contacted thought investigators who interview people suspected of child sexual abuse should be specifically trained in interview strategies that consider the nature of the relationship between victims and offenders. They indicated that this training would help interviewers design interrogation strategies and prepare them for the "explanations" and "rationalizations" abusers are likely to offer. Because abuser confessions may provide a wealth of corroborating evidence, interviews of suspected abusers require careful preparation and a thorough understanding of the abusers' motives and rationalizations.

The subject interview is a significant part of child sexual abuse investigations. Our review of closed case files disclosed that of the 30 subjects tried in court for sexually abusing children under age 12 years, 22 (73 percent) confessed during interrogation. The MCIOs were remarkably similar in this respect: the USACIDC rate was 75 percent; the NCIS rate was 71 percent; and the AFOSI rate was 73 percent. MCIO policy (Appendix E) and training (Appendix F) provide for developing interview strategies unique to child sexual abuse interrogations.

Overall, we believe that DoD, Military Department, and MCIO policies, training, and operational requirements are adequate to meet the challenge of subject interviews in child sexual abuse investigations.

F.   MCIO Support Resources

Armed Forces Center for Child Protection

In 1997, the Executive Board at National Naval Medical Center, Bethesda, Maryland, approved an initiative to establish the Armed Forces Center for Child Protection. AFCCP was created to provide consultative services for all DoD agencies needing objective medical expertise in suspected child maltreatment cases. At the time of our evaluation, the center was staffed with a director (a Navy captain), who is a board-certified pediatrician; a pediatrician (an Air Force lieutenant colonel); a nurse clinic manager (a Navy commander); a social worker funded by the Navy Family Advocacy Program; and a pediatric nurse practitioner funded by the Air Force Family Advocacy Program. AFCCP expected a third pediatrician (a Navy commander) to be assigned during the summer of 2001. AFCCP has a limited annual budget of $3,500, and agencies that request consultative service and testimony must fund travel and other expenses related to their requests.

According to AFCCP, the center's low funding level may impede its continued effectiveness. For example, AFCCP has neither a computer nor funds to acquire one for the pediatrician being assigned. Likewise, AFCCP does not currently have a computer projector to support lectures or enhanced software systems to expand into telemedicine using the World Wide Web. The center is actively seeking ways to encourage its largest clients, judge advocates and criminal investigators, to support additional needs.

AFCCP estimated that it had conducted more than 700 medical/legal reviews and given more than 1,000 lectures to multidisciplinary audiences (physicians, nurses, lawyers, and criminal investigators) since its establishment in 1997. The center's child sexual abuse topics have included medical examinations, sexual assault kits, interview strategies, child pornography, photo-documentation of injuries, long-term sequelae of adverse childhood experience, and normative sexual behavior in children.

MCIO program managers and child abuse specialists have enthusiastically praised the support they have received from AFCCP. They also advised that they regard AFCCP support as indispensable to their missions.

Internal Support Resources

The MCIOs each have internal resources for child sexual abuse investigations and have also encouraged agents to use outside resources. USACIDC and AFOSI policies require coordinating child sexual abuse investigations with specialists. The USACIDC requirement is relatively new (May 2000); the AFOSI requirement has existed for several years.

Army

In May 2000, the Army established a Sex Crimes/Child Abuse Monitorship management control program.[35] This program requires a senior agent at USACIDC battalion, group, or headquarters levels to monitor all sex crime and child abuse investigations to ensure uniformity in applying policy and technical procedures. USACIDC policies further require the monitors to have CAPIT, FASTA, FAST, and FACAT training. Additionally, as mentioned earlier, the CAPIT course is a required core competency for all USACIDC agents.

We met with two managers from USACIDC headquarters regarding the monitorship program. Each had a master's degree in forensic science and was directly involved in training monitors at the group and battalion levels. Although the program was too new for us to evaluate for actual results, when fully implemented it should enhance USACIDC criminal investigations involving child sexual abuse.

Navy

NCIS Domestic Violence Units investigate sex crimes and family violence for the Navy and the Marine Corps. These units are located in areas with strong Navy and Marine presence. NCIS guidance recommends specific training to deal with domestic violence, child abuse, and sex crimes. NCIS Special Agents in Charge, however, are responsible for managing their unit training based on the resources available to the

---

[35] Criminal Investigation Operational Procedures, CID Regulation 195-1, chapter 6, section V, January 1, 2000.

individual units.

As indicated in Appendix F, NCIS has follow-on training that specifically covers child sexual abuse for new agents. NCIS, however, does not have lesson plans, learning objectives, or instructor guides for the training. According to the program manager for child sexual abuse investigations, the Director, NCIS, "trusts the program managers to teach what the students need to know." Without specific lesson plans with learning objectives and instructor guides, we do not believe that NCIS can ensure consistency in the training and conformance with NCIS policy.

Air Force

The Air Force requires child sexual abuse investigations to be coordinated with an AFOSI Regional Forensic Science Consultant (RFC). RFCs are special agents assigned to geographic regions throughout the world to provide forensic science support to installation-level investigations. Each RFC has a master's degree in forensic science from George Washington University, Washington, D.C., and has completed an internship at the Cook County Medical Examiner's office in Chicago, Illinois, as well as DoD FACAT training. Additional training includes special agent laboratory protocols, bloodstain pattern interpretation, child abuse interview techniques, post-blast investigative techniques, and arson investigative techniques. The cases we reviewed identified RFC coordination in 19 of 22 Air Force cases (86 percent) involving child sexual abuse victims under the age of 12.[36]

The program manager for AFOSI child sexual abuse investigations has a doctorate with specialized postgraduate training in child development. She trains child sexual abuse investigators at the Air Force Special Investigations Academy. She also designed and conducts the Advanced Field Agent's Course on Child Forensic Interviews (referenced in Appendix F).

Overall, the MCIOs demonstrate a willingness to use outside assistance and to develop, conduct, or otherwise make training available to their agents to enhance their child sexual abuse investigations. The MCIOs also organize resources to meet interests unique to their Military Departments and effectively support their child sexual abuse investigations.

Recommendations

5. We recommend that the Under Secretary of Defense for personnel and readiness review current Armed Forces Center for Child Protection resources and determine whether they should be enhanced.

Management Comments. The USD(P&R) concurred and advised that his office

---

[36] According to the Forensic Science Program Manager, prior to a policy change in 2000, agents were not required to document RFC coordination in the investigative case file. Thus, actual RFC coordination may have been more than the number identified in cases reviewed.

had completed the review we recommended and was increasing AFCCP funding. In commenting on the final report, OUSD(P&R) should update this information to indicate the extent to which it increased AFCCP funding and the effective date.

6. **We recommend that the Naval Criminal Investigative Service develop coordinated lesson plans with learning objectives and instructor guides for its follow-on training for new agents to ensure consistency in training and conformance with governing policy.**

Management Comments. Navy concurred, advising that NCIS was developing lesson plans to enhance its training, and they should be completed by September 30, 2001. According to Navy, however, NCIS headquarters program managers are subject matter experts that the Director, NCIS, relies on to instruct contemporaneous practices, policy and trends that cannot be reflected in standardized lesson plans. As a result, Navy asked us to note that we did not find specific deficiencies in NCIS training, but that lesson plans would enhance consistency in training and conformance with governing policy. We so note. In commenting on the final report, Navy should provide a copy of the new lesson plans and identify their implementation date.

Appendix A. Summary of NAPA Recommendations

1. The MCIOs and DoD pay much more attention to investigations into child sexual abuse by implementing consistent policies, improving training, and examining the benefit of using specialized, child-oriented investigative techniques.

2. The MCIOs incorporate into their guidance and protocol a uniform set of investigative policies and techniques on child sexual abuse which are based on findings and recommendations by child psychology and sex crimes experts.

3. DoD and the MCIOs establish a trained cadre of child sex crimes investigators within each MCIO.

4. Basic training for all MCIO agents focus on child sexual abuse investigations as a distinct subject.

5. DoD and MCIOs maintain a strong support structure of dedicated competencies -- such as a program manager, regional specialists and domestic violence units -- to support investigations of child sex abuse.

Appendix B. Organizations with Effective Practices for Child Sexual Abuse Investigations

Arlington County Police Dept.
Sex Crimes/Youth Offenses/
Domestic Violence Unit
1425 N. Courthouse Road
Arlington, VA 22201

Dallas Police Dept.
Youth and Family Crimes Division
Child Abuse Unit
106 South Harwood Rd
Dallas, TX 75201

National Children's Advocacy Center.
200 Westside Square, Suite 700
Huntsville, AL 35801

Director, Family Assessment Clinic
University of Michigan
Ann Arbor, MI 48104

Headquarters, FBI
Crimes Against Children Unit, and
National Center for the Analysis
of Violent Crime
935 Pennsylvania Ave., N.W.
Washington, DC 20535

New York Police Dept.
Special Victims Liaison Unit
1 Police Plaza
New York, NY 10023

San Diego Police Dept.
Child Abuse Unit
1401 Broadway
San Diego, CA 92101

Virginia Beach Police Dept.
Special Victims Unit
Municipal Center
Virginia Beach, VA 23456

Appendix C. Survey of Law Enforcement Approaches to Investigating Allegations of Child Sexual Abuse (Concept Validation)

Allegations of child sex abuse present special challenges to the law enforcement officers who must investigate them. Police officials, medical personnel, and child welfare professionals each have an important interest in these matters. Sometimes it is hard to tell exactly who should play what role at what point because, although these organizational interests may overlap, they are *not* identical.

We want to identify the proper roles and responsibilities the criminal investigative organizations within the Department of Defense should play in child sex abuse cases. These organizations consist of the U.S. Army Criminal Investigations Command (CID); the Navy Criminal Investigative Service (NCIS); and the Air Force Office of Special Investigations (AFOSI). These organizations investigate felony-level crimes committed within their jurisdiction and function much like the detective division of a large police department. They are all heavily involved in child sex abuse investigations.

To help us better define their role in child sex abuse investigations, we have contacted a number of civilian law enforcement and child advocacy organizations. As a result, we have identified a number of areas that appear to be of major significance. This questionnaire serves two purposes. First, it is a form of feedback to let you know the issues that were reported to us. Second, it gives you the opportunity to let us know which concepts you consider to be the most important.

Please take a few minutes to complete the questionnaire. Because of the select number of agencies to which this is being addressed, your response to us is very important.

In each of the questions you are provided a series of choices. Please select the one choice you believe most accurately represents your perspective.

***

1. The initial focus of law enforcement in an allegation of child sex abuse should be to determine if a crime has been committed.

☐ Strongly agree   ☐ Agree   ☐ No Opinion   ☐ Disagree   ☐ Strongly Disagree

2. Non-law enforcement agencies should participate in gathering evidence to be used in support of prosecution in child sex abuse cases.

☐ Strongly agree ☐ Agree ☐ No Opinion ☐ Disagree ☐ Strongly Disagree

3. The primary focus of a Child Protective Service in responding to reports of child sex abuse should be to facilitate treatment for the physical and emotional harm the victim has suffered.

☐ Strongly agree ☐ Agree ☐ No Opinion ☐ Disagree ☐ Strongly Disagree

4. Multi-disciplinary teams should have jointly written and mutually approved protocols that outline the structure, participants, and responsibilities of the team and its members.

☐ Strongly agree ☐ Agree ☐ No Opinion ☐ Disagree ☐ Strongly Disagree

5. Multi-disciplinary teams investigating allegations of child sex abuse should establish clear rules for sharing evidence and information in specific cases.

☐ Strongly agree ☐ Agree ☐ No Opinion ☐ Disagree ☐ Strongly Disagree

6. Law enforcement personnel who interview child sex abuse victims should have training on principles of child development, to include their psycho-sexual development.

☐ Strongly agree ☐ Agree ☐ No Opinion ☐ Disagree ☐ Strongly Disagree

7. Law enforcement personnel who interview child sex abuse victims should have training on how children think and use language.

☐ Strongly agree ☐ Agree ☐ No Opinion ☐ Disagree ☐ Strongly Disagree

8. Law enforcement personnel who interview child sex abuse victims should have training on strategies to reduce suggestibility during the interview process.

☐ Strongly agree ☐ Agree ☐ No Opinion ☐ Disagree ☐ Strongly Disagree

9. Law enforcement personnel who interview child sex abuse victims should have training on how to recognize signs of sex abuse.

☐ Strongly agree ☐ Agree ☐ No Opinion ☐ Disagree ☐ Strongly Disagree

10. Law enforcement personnel who interview child sex abuse victims should have training on how to build rapport with children according to their age.

☐ Strongly agree ☐ Agree ☐ No Opinion ☐ Disagree ☐ Strongly Disagree

11. Law enforcement personnel who interview child sex abuse victims should have training on how to assess the child's level of emotional development.

☐ Strongly agree　　☐ Agree　　☐ No Opinion　　☐ Disagree　　☐ Strongly Disagree

12. Law enforcement personnel who interview child sex abuse victims should have training on how to assess the child's comprehension level.

☐ Strongly agree　　☐ Agree　　☐ No Opinion　　☐ Disagree　　☐ Strongly Disagree

13. Law enforcement personnel who interview child sex abuse victims under the age of 8 or who are developmentally disabled should have training on interview strategies that assess the child's competency.

☐ Strongly agree　　☐ Agree　　☐ No Opinion　　☐ Disagree　　☐ Strongly Disagree

14. Law enforcement personnel who interview child sex abuse victims should have training on the profiles or seduction strategies commonly used by child sex abuse offenders.

☐ Strongly agree　　☐ Agree　　☐ No Opinion　　☐ Disagree　　☐ Strongly Disagree

15. Law enforcement personnel who interview child sex abuse victims should have training on interview strategies that consider the relationship between the victim and the offender.

☐ Strongly agree　　☐ Agree　　☐ No Opinion　　☐ Disagree　　☐ Strongly Disagree

16. Law enforcement personnel who interview child sex abuse victims should have training on how to assess the victim's sense of guilt, shame, or embarrassment.

☐ Strongly agree　　☐ Agree　　☐ No Opinion　　☐ Disagree　　☐ Strongly Disagree

17. Anatomically detailed dolls used during the interview of victims of child sex abuse should only be used by trained personnel.

☐ Strongly agree　　☐ Agree　　☐ No Opinion　　☐ Disagree　　☐ Strongly Disagree

18. Anatomically detailed drawings used during the interview of victims of child sex abuse should only be used by trained personnel.

☐ Strongly agree　　☐ Agree　　☐ No Opinion　　☐ Disagree　　☐ Strongly Disagree

19. Freehand drawings used during the interview of victims of child sex abuse should only be used by trained personnel.

☐ Strongly agree   ☐ Agree   ☐ No Opinion   ☐ Disagree   ☐ Strongly Disagree

20. All interviews of victims in child sex abuse cases should be documented by video recordings.

☐ Strongly agree   ☐ Agree   ☐ No Opinion   ☐ Disagree   ☐ Strongly Disagree

21. It is preferable that properly trained law enforcement personnel conduct the forensic interview of the victim in a child sex abuse investigation.

☐ Strongly agree   ☐ Agree   ☐ No Opinion   ☐ Disagree   ☐ Strongly Disagree

22. It is preferable that only one interviewer be present in the interview room during the forensic interview of the victim of child sex abuse.

☐ Strongly agree   ☐ Agree   ☐ No Opinion   ☐ Disagree   ☐ Strongly Disagree

23. Law enforcement personnel who interrogate alleged child sex abuse offenders should have training for interview strategies that consider the nature of the relationship between the victim and the offender.

☐ Strongly agree   ☐ Agree   ☐ No Opinion   ☐ Disagree   ☐ Strongly Disagree

24. Law enforcement personnel who investigate child sex abuse should have training on the evidence to be obtained from the medical examination of victims.

☐ Strongly agree   ☐ Agree   ☐ No Opinion   ☐ Disagree   ☐ Strongly Disagree

25. The organization <u>most</u> responsible for identifying all potential victims and witnesses in child sex abuse cases is:

☐ Police ☐ Child Protective Services ☐ Prosecutor ☐ Medical/Mental Health
☐ Other: _____

26. Which organization should have the <u>primary</u> responsibility for gathering evidence in support of potential prosecution in child sex abuse investigations?

☐ Police   ☐ Child Protective Services   ☐ Prosecutor   ☐ Other:

27. Ensuring the immediate safety of juvenile victims should be the responsibility of:

☐ Police ☐ Child Protective Services ☐ Prosecutor ☐ Non-offending parents or Caretaker
☐ Other _____

28. Assessing the degree of environmental and human risk facing child victims in sex abuse cases should be the responsibility of which of:

☐ Police ☐ Child Protective Services ☐ Prosecutor ☐ Medical Personnel
☐ Other: _____

29. Who should have <u>primary</u> responsibility for determining the extent of physical and emotional harm suffered by the victims of child sex abuse?

☐ Police ☐ Child Protective Services ☐ Medical and allied health sciences personnel
☐ Non-Offending Parent or Caretaker ☐ Other: _____

30. What do you believe is the best approach to managing allegations of child sex abuse?

☐ For the police to complete their investigation first; ☐ For Child Protective Services to assess the victim before referring the matter to the police; or ☐ For the police and Child Protective Services to form a multi-disciplinary team and work the issue together.

31. The *initial* interview of a potential child sex abuse victim should be conducted by:

☐ Police (to see if a crime has been committed) ☐ Medical personnel (to see if any physical harm can be detected) Child Protective Services (to assess the extent to which the child is at risk) ☐ Teacher or school counselor ☐ Other:

32. Where do you think is the best place to interview a victim of child sex abuse?

☐ In the interview room of a police department ☐ Any safe and emotionally neutral environment ☐ In a medical environment (hospital, clinic, doctor's office, etc). ☐ In the offices of Child Protective Services ☐ Where the person having custody of the child wants the interview to take place.

Appendix D. Summary Results From Statistical Random Sample

Child Sexual Abuse Investigations

	0-2 Yrs		3-5 Yrs		6-8 Yrs		9-11 Yrs		Under 12 Yrs		12-14 Yrs		15-17 Yrs		Over 11 Yrs		Total	
	No	%	No	%	No	%	No	%	No	%	No	%	No	%	No	%	No	%
No. Cases	5	3%	29	19%	27	18%	22	14%	83	54%	45	29%	25	16%	70	46%	153	100%
No. Subjects	5	3%	29	19%	27	17%	23	15%	84	54%	46	30%	25	16%	71	46%	155	100%
Active Duty	3	60%	24	83%	21	78%	21	91%	69	82%	34	74%	21	84%	55	77%	124	80%
Dependent		0%	4	14%	2	7%	2	9%	8	10%	5	11%	3	12%	8	11%	16	10%
DoD Civilian		0%		0%		0%		0%	0	0%	3	7%		0%	3	4%	3	2%
Non-DoD	2	40%	1	3%	3	11%		0%	6	7%	4	9%	1	4%	5	7%	11	7%
Unknown					1	4%			1	1%					0	0%	1	1%
Total	5	100%	29	100%	27	100%	23	100%	84	100%	46	100%	25	100%	71	100%	155	100%
No. Victims	7		34		32		29		102		55		30		85		187	
Male	1	14%	5	15%	6	19%	6	21%	18	18%	6	11%	2	7%	8	9%	26	14%
Female	6	86%	29	85%	26	81%	23	79%	84	82%	49	89%	28	93%	77	91%	161	86%
Total	7	100%	34	100%	32	100%	29	100%	102	100%	55	100%	30	100%	85	100%	187	100%
Average Victim Age																		
When Abuse Began	1.6		4.1		6.9		10				13		15				9.9	
When Interviewed	2.3		5.6		8.4		12				14		16				11	
Difference	0.4		1.5		1.4		2.1				0.5		0.5				1.1	
Was the Victim Part of the Military Community?																		
Yes	6	86%	33	97%	28	88%	22	76%	89	87%	37	67%	19	63%	56	66%	145	78%
No	1	14%	1	3%	4	13%	7	24%	13	13%	18	33%	11	37%	29	34%	42	22%
Total	7	100%	34	100%	32	100%	29	100%	102	100%	55	100%	30	100%	85	100%	187	100%
What Was the Subject's Relationship to the Victim?																		
Parent	1	14%	14	41%	11	34%	11	38%	37	36%	4	7%		0%	4	5%	41	22%
Step-Parent		0%	8	24%	5	16%	8	28%	21	21%	7	13%	4	13%	11	13%	32	17%
Sibling/Step-Sibling		0%		0%		0%		0%	0	0%	1	2%		0%	1	1%	1	1%
Other Relative	1	14%	1	3%	2	6%	3	10%	7	7%	1	2%	1	3%	2	2%	9	5%
Parent Love Interest	1	14%		0%	2	6%		0%	3	3%		0%		0%	0	0%	3	2%
Friend or Neighbor	3	43%	7	21%	10	31%	5	17%	25	25%	22	40%	17	57%	39	46%	64	34%
Paid Caretaker		0%	2	6%		0%		0%	2	2%		0%		0%	0	0%	2	1%
Other	1	14%	2	6%	2	6%	2	7%	7	7%	20	36%	7	23%	27	32%	34	18%
Unknown		0%		0%		0%		0%	0	0%		0%	1	3%	1	1%	1	1%
Total	7	100%	34	100%	32	100%	29	100%	102	100%	55	100%	30	100%	85	100%	187	100%
Type of Abuse Alleged																		
Fondling	4	57%	24	71%	26	81%	20	69%	74	73%	28	51%	12	40%	40	47%	114	61%
Intercourse		0%	4	12%	2	6%	2	7%	8	8%	25	45%	18	60%	43	51%	51	27%
Sodomy		0%	12	35%	4	13%	6	21%	22	22%	7	13%	7	23%	14	16%	36	19%
Digital Manipulation	2	29%	7	21%	4	13%	6	21%	19	19%	7	13%	8	27%	15	18%	34	18%
Visual Stimulation		0%	1	3%		0%	5	17%	6	6%	6	11%	1	3%	7	8%	13	7%
Visual Exploitation		0%	1	3%	4	13%	3	10%	8	8%	2	4%		0%	2	2%	10	5%
Foreign Object Insertion	1	14%		0%		0%		0%	1	1%	1	2%		0%	1	1%	2	1%
Other		0%		0%	2	6%	4	14%	6	6%	6	11%	5	17%	11	13%	17	9%
Total	7	100%	49	144%	42	131%	46	159%	144	141%	82	149%	51	170%	133	156%	277	148%

	Victim Age																	
	0-2 Yrs		3-5 Yrs		6-8 Yrs		9-11 Yrs		Under 12 Yrs		12-14 Yrs		15-17 Yrs		Over 11 Yrs		Total	
	No	%	No	%	No	%	No	%	No	%	No	%	No	%	No	%	No	%
Where Did the Alleged Abuse Occur?																		
On/Off Mil Installation																		
On	5	71%	25	74%	19	59%	11	38%	60	59%	33	60%	20	67%	53	62%	113	60%
On and Off		0%	2	6%	2	6%	4	14%	8	8%	6	11%	4	13%	10	12%	18	10%
Off	2	29%	7	21%	11	34%	14	48%	34	33%	16	29%	6	20%	22	26%	56	30%
Total	7	100%	34	100%	32	100%	29	100%	102	100%	55	100%	30	100%	85	100%	187	100%
Location																		
Vict/Subj Residence	2	29%	17	50%	14	44%	15	52%	48	47%	17	31%	5	17%	22	26%	70	37%
Victim Residence	4	57%	5	15%	4	13%	1	3%	14	14%	3	5%	1	3%	4	5%	18	10%
Subject Residence	1	14%	10	29%	9	28%	11	38%	31	30%	15	27%	8	27%	23	27%	54	29%
Other		0%	2	6%	5	16%	2	7%	9	9%	20	36%	16	53%	36	42%	45	24%
Total	7	100%	34	100%	32	100%	29	100%	102	100%	55	100%	30	100%	85	100%	187	100%
Which Justice System Adjudicated the Case?																		
UCMJ	3	60%	24	83%	20	74%	20	87%	67	80%	33	72%	22	88%	55	77%	122	79%
Civilian	2	40%	5	17%	7	26%	3	13%	17	20%	13	28%	3	12%	16	23%	33	21%
Total	5	100%	29	100%	27	100%	23	100%	84	100%	46	100%	25	100%	71	100%	155	100%

* **Age when abuse started**

Notes:

This table includes overall victim and subject data. In cases where one subject involves more than one victim, subject data are limited to a "one-count" to avoid duplication.

Appendix E. Policy, Regulation, or Program Guidance Addressing Challenges Unique to Child Sexual Abuse Investigations

Challenge Area	Policy Addresses Challenge Area			
	DoD[1]	Army[2]	Navy[3]	Air Force[4]
Multidisciplinary teams				
Using multidisciplinary teams	Yes	Yes	Yes	Yes
Sharing information and evidence	Yes	Yes	Yes	Yes
Coordinating actions	Yes	Yes	Yes	Yes
Interview of child victims				
Recognizing child development parameters	No	Yes	Yes	Yes
Reducing suggestibility	Yes	Yes	Yes	Yes
Using anatomical dolls	No	Yes	Yes	No
Using anatomical drawings	No	Yes	Yes	No
Using freehand drawings	Yes	Yes	Yes	Yes
Using child-friendly or neutral interview locations	No	Yes	Yes	Yes
Recording interviews	No	Yes	Yes	Yes
Medical examination				
Obtaining evidence from medical examination	Yes	Yes	Yes	Yes
Interview of accused				
Using appropriate interview strategies	No	Yes	Yes	Yes

[1] DoD Directive 6400.1, Family Advocacy Program, June 23, 1992; DoD Instruction, 6400.3, Family Advocacy Command Assistance Team, February 3, 1989, and the DoD Family Advocacy Command Assistance Team Handbook.

[2] Army Regulation Army Regulation 608-18, The Army Family Advocacy Program, September 1, 1995; CID Regulation 195-1, Criminal Investigation Operational Procedures, January 1, 2000; CID Pamphlet 195-10, Crime Scene Handbook, June 30, 1999, and Field Manual 19-20, Law Enforcement Investigations, November 1985.

[3] Chief of Naval Operations Instruction (OPNAVINST) 1752.2A, Family Advocacy Program, July 17, 1996; Naval Criminal Investigative Service Manual 3 (NCIS 3), and American Prosecutors Research Institute manual, Investigation and Prosecution of Child Abuse, Second Edition, adopted as NCIS investigative policy at NCIS 3, Chapter 34, paragraph 3.5.

[4] Air Force Instruction (AFI) 40-301, Family Advocacy, July 22, 1994; AFI 51-201, Administration of Military Justice, November 2, 1999; AFI 71-101, Vol 1, Criminal Investigations, December 1, 1999; Air Force Office of Special Investigations Manual, (AFOSIMAN) Vol 2, 71-103, AFOSI Forensic Sciences, October 23, 1995; Air Force Office of Special Investigations Instruction (AFOSII) 71-105, Investigations, December 1, 1998; AFOSII 71-107, Processing Investigative Matters, March 15, 2000; AFOSIMAN 71-118, General Investigative Methods, December 21, 1998; AFOSIMAN 71-122, Criminal Investigations, August 30, 1996; AFOSI Handbook 71-124, Crime Scene Handbook, March 13, 1998.

Appendix F. Training That Addresses Challenges Unique to Child Sexual Abuse Investigations

Challenge Area	Training Addresses Challenge Area						
	DoD	Army		Navy		Air Force	
	FACAT	ASAC	CAPIT	NCIS	APSAC	AFOSI	AFACCFI
Multidisciplinary teams							
Using multidisciplinary teams	Yes	Yes	Yes	Yes	Yes	Yes	Yes
Sharing information and evidence	Yes	Yes	Yes	Yes	Yes	Yes	Yes
Coordinating actions	Yes	Yes	Yes	Yes	Yes	Yes	Yes
Interview of child victims							
Recognizing child development parameters	Yes	Yes	Yes	Yes	Yes	Yes	Yes
Reducing suggestibility	Yes	Yes	No	Yes	Yes	Yes	Yes
Building rapport	Yes	Yes	Yes	Yes	Yes	Yes	Yes
Recognizing signs of sex abuse	Yes	No	Yes	Yes	Yes	No	Yes
Using anatomical dolls	Yes	Yes	Yes	Yes	Yes	Yes	Yes
Using anatomical drawings	Yes	Yes	No	Yes	Yes	Yes	Yes
Using freehand drawings	Yes	Yes	Yes	Yes	Yes	Yes	Yes
Using child-friendly or neutral interview locations	Yes	Yes	Yes	Yes	Yes	Yes	Yes
Recording interviews	Yes	Yes	Yes	Yes	Yes	Yes	Yes
Identifying other possible victims	Yes	Yes	No	Yes	Yes	Yes	Yes
Medical examination							
Obtaining evidence from medical examination	Yes	Yes	Yes	Yes	Yes	Yes	Yes
Interview of accused							
Using appropriate interview strategies	Yes	Yes	Yes	Yes	No	Yes	No

AFACCFI   AFOSI Advanced Field Agent's Course on Child Forensic Interviews
AFOSI   AFOSI (Initial and follow-on training. All AFOSI agents attend this training.)
APSAC   American Professional Society on Abuse of Children
ASAC   USACIDC Apprentice Special Agent Course
CAPIT   Child Abuse Prevention and Investigative Techniques
FACAT   Family Advocacy Command Assistant Team
NCIS   NCIS (Initial and follow-on training. All NCIS agents attend this training. Course presentation slides identified coverage as shown in the table. However, NCIS did not have written learning objectives, lesson plans, or instructor guides for the training.)

Appendix G. Report Distribution

Office of the Secretary of Defense

Under Secretary of Defense (Personnel and Readiness)*

Under Secretary of Defense (Comptroller)

Assistant Secretary of Defense (Force Management Policy)

Deputy Comptroller (Program/Budget), Office of the Under Secretary of Defense (Comptroller)*

Deputy Chief Financial Officer, Accounting Policy Directorate, Office of the Under Secretary of Defense (Comptroller)

Department of the Army

Assistant Secretary of the Army (Financial Management and Comptroller)*

Inspector General, Department of the Army*

U.S. Army Audit Agency

Commanding General, U.S. Army Criminal Investigation Command*

Commandant, U.S. Army Military Police School*

Department of the Navy

Naval Inspector General*

Naval Audit Service

Director, Naval Criminal Investigative Service*

Department of the Air Force

Assistant Secretary of the Air Force (Financial Management and Comptroller)*

Inspector General, Department of the Air Force*

Auditor General, Department of the Air Force

Commander, Air Force Office of Special Investigations*

Other Defense Organizations

Director, Defense Contract Audit Agency

Director, Defense Intelligence Agency

*Recipient of draft report

Director, National Security Agency
Inspector General, National Security Agency
Commandant, Defense Acquisition University
Director, Defense Criminal Investigative Service*

Non-Defense Federal Organizations and Individuals

None

Congressional Committees and Subcommittees, Chairman and Ranking Minority Member

Senate Committee on Appropriations

Senate Subcommittee on Defense, Committee on Appropriations

Senate Committee on Armed Services

Senate Committee on Governmental Affairs

House Committee on Appropriations

House Subcommittee on Defense, Committee on Appropriations

House Committee on Armed Services

House Committee on Government Reform

House Subcommittee on National Security Veterans Affairs, and International Relations, Committee on Government Reform

House Subcommittee on Government Efficiency, Financial Management, and Intergovernmental Relations, Committee on Government Reform

House Subcommittee on Technology and Procurement Policy, Committee on Government Reform

*Recipient of draft report

UNDER SECRETARY OF DEFENSE
4000 DEFENSE PENTAGON
WASHINGTON, D.C. 20301-4000

SEP 27 2001

PERSONNEL AND
READINESS

MEMORANDUM FOR INSPECTOR GENERAL, DEPARTMENT OF DEFENSE

SUBJECT: Evaluation of Criminal Investigative Organizations Policies, Practices, and Procedures for Investigating Child Sexual Abuse (Project No. 9850011K)

Thank you for providing the opportunity to review the draft report. I concur with the study's findings and recommendations. In accordance with recommendation 5 on page 20, a review of the current resources available for the Armed Forces Center for Child Protection was conducted. The review determined that additional resources were needed for the Center, and I am pleased to inform you that they will be made available to the Center as soon as possible.

David S. C. Chu

DEPARTMENT OF THE ARMY
OFFICE OF THE DEPUTY CHIEF OF STAFF FOR OPERATIONS AND PLANS
400 ARMY PENTAGON
WASHINGTON OC 20310-0400

REPLY TO
ATTENTION OF

1 8 OCT 2001

DAMO-ODL

MEMORANDUM THRU ~~DEPUTY CHIEF OF STAFF FOR OPERATIONS AND PLANS~~
DIRECTOR OF THE ARMY STAFF
ASSISTANT SECRETARY OF THE ARMY (MANPOWER AND
RESERVE AFFAIRS)

FOR INSPECTOR GENERAL, DEPARTMENT OF DEFENSE, DEPUTY ASSISTANT
INSPECTOR GENERAL, CRIMINAL INVESTIGATIVE POLICY AND
OVERSIGHT

SUBJECT: Draft Report on the Evaluation of Criminal Investigative Organizations
Policies, Practices, and Procedures for Investigations Involving Child Sexual Abuse
(Project No. 9950011K)

1. Concur with subject report. Our comments are provided in the enclosure.

2. In summary, the U.S. Army Criminal Investigation Command (USACIDC) completed
100 percent legal coordination on the sample cases for which they had investigative
authority and responsibility. The subject report does not comment on the timeliness of
incidents being reported, which may result in lost opportunity to gather medical
evidence. The alternative in such cases is often an invasive medical examination which
could further traumatize the victim. Statistical data involves methodology for collecting
data and analysis of the data. We have provided comments on that aspect of the
report.

3. The point of contact is Mr. Jeffery Porter, (703) 695-8823.

Encl

PETER W. CHIARELLI
Brigadier General, GS
Director of Operations,
Readiness and Mobilization

Printed on Recycled Paper

H-2

Concur with recommendations #1 and #2 with the following comments:

a. Recommendation #1:

(1) The information concerning the legal coordination in Tables 3 and 4 of the report are not consistent with a subsequent re-evaluation completed by the USACIDC. The re-evaluation determined that legal coordination was completed for 100 percent of the sample cases. In fives cases (0507-97-CID013, 1306-97-CID034, 0125-98-CID063, 0069-98-CID023, and 0869-99-CID025), coordination was completed with a Special Assistant United States Attorney or the Assistant United States Attorney. Another case (0050-99-CID093), was referred to the Federal Bureau of Investigation (FBI), an action that would not require legal coordination as follow-on investigative work was to be done by the FBI. The subject report should be modified to reflect the proper percentage of USACIDC legal coordination.

(2) Tables 3 and 4 of the report indicate USACIDC's use of medical coordination percentage as 45 percent and 22 percent respectively. This may not be an accurate representation since the report does not indicate the timeliness of the reporting of the incident. If the incident was not reported in a timely manner and the medical evidence has already been lost, a subsequent invasive medical examination could further traumatize the victim. Instead of implying that medical coordination was always needed, the report should have examined and commented on this aspect of the investigative process. The report should be modified to reflect that medical coordination might not always be required or conducted if the incident was not reported in a timely manner.

b. Recommendation #2:

(1) Documentation on page 5 of the report reflects 102 victims (55 percent of the total) involved children below the age of 12," but on page 13, the report states 79 victims of child sexual abuse were below 12 years of age." The report should be modified to reflect whichever number (102 or 79) is the proper number of victims of child abuse below 12 years of age.

(2) The report indicated in Table 5 that the relatively low overall population of interviews conducted by specially trained agents was disproportionately influenced by the USACIDC totals, where specially trained agents conducted only 25 percent of the interviews. An additional document received from the Department of Defense Inspector General (DODIG) identified the agents who were considered specially trained at the time they conducted child interviews. That document indicated out of the 16 victims interviewed, that 7 not 4 agents (1997 had 3 interviews conducted by a specially trained agent not 0 as reported) were considered specially trained prior to interviewing the victims. This is 44 percent and not the reported 25 percent. Also, the four agents who were not specially trained had a social worker assist in the interview. These interviews should also be considered as specially trained interviews since a specially trained individual assisted in the interview. This would make the number of specially

trained interviews 69 percent instead of the reported 25 percent. The report should be adjusted to reflect the appropriate percentage.

(3) When establishing whether or not an agent was considered as having specialized training in interviewing of the victim, the individual backgrounds of the agents were not evaluated. Some agents have received specialized training in child development and training in college courses, unit training or local/regional discretionary training with other law enforcement agencies. Every USACIDC agent receives twelve hours of child interview specific training in the apprentice special agent course. Additionally, 480 USACIDC agents have received advanced specialty training since 1997. Giving full credit for that training might well increase the training percentages discussed in the above paragraph. According to Recommendation #6 of the report, the DODIG could not evaluate the Naval Criminal Investigative Service (NCIS) follow-on specialty training course, yet it gave the NCIS agents credit for being specially trained. The report should also specifically reflect that each USACIDC agent receives child interview training in their initial training. If the Navy training cannot be evaluated to the same degree as the USACIDC and Office of Special Investigations training courses, then some comment in connection with Table 5 should be made to that effect. It is believed the statistical sampling was flawed and the process utilized may need to be refined for future studies. Of the 1,725 total cases done by the Department of Defense Major Criminal Investigative Organizations (MCIOs) over a 3 year period, 957 (or 55 percent) were USACIDC cases with 45 percent from the other 2 MCIOs (Navy and Air Force). Yet, each MCIO had about the same number of cases reviewed. Presumably, a statistical sampling would have resulted in twice the number of USACIDC cases being reviewed when compared to the other MCIOs. Based on the report's fact that USACIDC investigates about twice as many child assaults as the other MCIOs, request an additional recommendation be made in the report to reflect that USACIDC should receive twice the number of training allocations as the other MCIOs.

c. Recommendation #3. The U.S. Army Military Police School (USAMPS) has lesson plans for child interviews and military police investigator child interview portions of training. USAMPS also has lesson plans for the child interview and children's language portions of Child Abuse Prevention and Investigative Techniques training course. These lesson plans were for guest instructors listing the Terminal Learning Objectives and requirements for training. Due to the fact that they were guest instructors and are subject to change from year-to-year and the fact that USAMPS brings in professionals and experts in their field of training, it was not appropriate to prescribe their lesson plans or presentations. USAMPS has stopped using those experts and is converting those lesson plans into one lesson plan to be taught by USAMPS Subject Matter Expert. The new lesson plan incorporates all information required by the DODIG assessment.

2

DEPARTMENT OF THE NAVY
OFFICE OF THE ASSISTANT SECRETARY
(MANPOWER AND RESERVE AFFAIRS)
1000 NAVY PENTAGON
WASHINGTON, D.C. 20350-1000

DEC ṿ 3 2001

MEMORANDUM FOR INSPECTOR GENERAL, DEPARTMENT OF DEFENSE

SUBJECT: Draft Report on the Evaluation of Criminal
Investigative Organizations Policies, Practices, and
Procedures for Investigating Child Sex Abuse
(Project 9850011K)

The Department of the Navy has reviewed the subject report
and, except as noted below, concurs with the findings and
recommendations. The position and recommendations of the Naval
Criminal Investigative Service, as set forth in Attachment (1),
are favorably endorsed and incorporated into the Department of
the Navy's position. The following comments on the report's six
recommendations are provided.

1. Recommendation 1: CONCUR.

2. Recommendation 2: CONCUR.

3. Recommendation 3: NO COMMENT

4. Recommendation 4: NO COMMENT.

5. Recommendation 5: CONCUR.

6. Recommendation 6: CONCUR WITH COMMENT. NCIS has
developed lesson plans to enhance training provided by
experienced instructors.

If additional information or assistance is needed, the NCIS
point of contact is Ms. Veronica McCarthy, Assistant Director of
Inspections, (202) 433-8830.

Thomas V. Colella
Principal Deputy
Assistant Secretary of the Navy
(Manpower & Reserve Affairs)

Attachment 1: Headquarters, NCIS memorandum of 30 October 2001

DEPARTMENT OF THE NAVY

HEADQUARTERS
NAVAL CRIMINAL INVESTIGATIVE SERVICE
WASHINGTON NAVY YARD BLDG 111
716 SICARD STREET SE
WASHINGTON DC 20388-5380

30 October 2001

MEMORANDUM FOR THE INSPECTOR GENERAL, DEPARTMENT OF DEFENSE

FROM: Director, Naval Criminal Investigative Service
      Prepared by: Susan Raser, Special Agent, (202) 433-9236

SUBJECT: Draft Report on the Evaluation of Criminal Investigative Organizations
         Policies, Practices, and Procedures for Investigating Child Sex Abuse
         (Project 9850011K)

PURPOSE: To provide comments on the findings and recommendations from the subject
         named report

SUMMARY OF RECOMMENDATIONS:
1) The MCIOs, during reoccurring inspections, staff assistance and oversight visits to
   field locations, verify that criminal investigators involved in child sexual abuse
   investigations are in all such cases participating in multidisciplinary teams,
   coordinating overall investigative activities, and sharing information throughout the
   investigations.
2) USACIDC, through its internal oversight program, give special emphasis to assuring
   that USACIDC agents who interview victims of child sexual abuse have been trained
   to interview children.
3) USACIDC adopt a lesson plan with learning objectives and instructor guide for its
   block of instruction dealing with child interviews in the CAPIT training program.
4) AFOSI should incorporate into its written policy that AFOSI agents should not use
   anatomically detailed dolls during the interview of children.
5) The Under Secretary of Defense (P&R) review current Armed Forces Center for
   Child Protection (AFCCP) resources and determine if they should be enhanced.
6) NCIS should develop coordinated lesson plans with learning objectives and instructor
   guides for its follow-on training for basic agents to assure consistency in training and
   conformance with governing policy.

STATEMENT OF NCIS POSITION:
NCIS concurs with the recommendation that the MCIOs should conduct inspections to
verify that child sex abuse cases are being investigated using a multidisciplinary team
approach. NCIS already inspects for this during NCISHQ inspections of field elements.
NCIS also concurs that USACIDC should provide specialized training to agents who
interview child sex abuse victims. AFOSI and NCIS already provide specialized training
to agents who conduct interviews of child sex abuse victims. The MCIOs conduct
reciprocal leads for each other and training of agents should be consistent throughout

DoD. NCIS concurs that the Under Secretary of Defense (P&R) should enhance the resources for the AFCCP. NCIS has provided equipment to the center and maintains that equipment because of lack of direct funding to the AFCCP.

NCIS concurs with comment that we should develop lesson plans with learning objectives and instructor guides for child sex abuse training. We believe lesson plans are an excellent tool for instruction and we are currently developing lesson plans for this training. However, it is the NCIS position that lesson plans cannot take the place of an experienced instructor who can instruct on contemporaneous practices, policies and trends that may not be reflected in a standardized lesson plan. Planned Action: Lesson plans are currently being developed and should be complete by 30 September 2001.

NCIS has no position on the recommendations that USACIDC should adopt a lesson plan and learning objectives for child interview training, and that AFOSI should have written policy directing its agents not to use anatomically detailed dolls. Each of these recommendations is exclusive to another MCIOs' policy and operating procedures.

A summary of recommendations and the NCIS position is attached as enclosure (1).

ENCLOSURE
(1) Summary of Recommendations and NCIS Position

VERONICA MCCARTHY
By Direction

Summary of Recommendations and NCIS Position

1. The Military Criminal Investigative Organizations, during recurring inspection, staff assistance and oversight visits to field locations, verify that criminal investigators involved in child sexual abuse investigations are in all such cases participating in multidisciplinary teams, coordinating overall investigative activities, and sharing information throughout the investigations.

    CONCUR

    Comments: NCIS is in compliance with this recommendation and routinely inspects field locations to ensure that investigations are coordinated with the appropriate social service agencies. Yearly field office evaluations conducted by NCISHQ are prepared that include evaluation of working relationships with members of multidisciplinary teams.

2. We recommend that US Army Criminal Investigation Command, through its internal oversight program, give special emphasis to assuring that USACIDC agents who interview victims of child sexual abuse have been trained to interview children.

    CONCUR

    Comments: NCIS, AFOSI and USACIDC conduct reciprocal leads in areas where each agency is not represented. CID agents interviewing children in reference to an NCIS investigation should have specialized training in child interviewing.

3. We recommend that the US Army Criminal Investigation Command adopt a lesson plan with learning objectives and instructor guide for its block of instruction dealing with child interviews in the Child Abuse Prevention and Investigative Techniques training program.

    NO POSITION

4. We recommend that since AFOSI trains its agents not to use anatomically detailed dolls during the interview of children, such guidance should be incorporated in its written policy.

    NO POSITION

5. We recommend that Under Secretary of Defense (P&R) review current Armed Forces Center for Child Protection resources and determine if they should be enhanced.

    CONCUR

6. We recommend that the Naval Criminal Investigative Service develop coordinated lesson plans with learning objectives and instructor guides for its follow-on training for basic agents to assure consistency in training and conformance with governing policy.

    CONCUR WITH COMMENT

    Comments: We believe lesson plans are an excellent tool for instruction, but the headquarters program managers are the director's subject matter experts and can instruct on contemporaneous practices, policy and trends which may not be reflected in a standardized lesson plan. Request that it be noted in the report that no deficiencies were noted in the training provided by NCIS but that lesson plans would *enhance* ~~assure~~ consistency in training and conformance with governing policy.

    Planned action: Lesson plans are currently being developed and should be complete by 30Sep01.

DEPARTMENT OF THE AIR FORCE
AIR FORCE OFFICE OF SPECIAL INVESTIGATIONS
ANDREWS AIR FORCE BASE MD

MEMORANDUM FOR CHARLES W. BEARDALL
OFFICE OF THE DEPUTY ASSISTANT INSPECTOR GENERAL
FOR CRIMINAL INVESTIGATIVE POLICY AND OVERSIGHT
ROOM 944, 400 ARMY NAVY DRIVE
ARLINGTON, VA 22202-2884

FROM: AFOSI/CC
1535 Command Drive
Suite C301
Andrews AFB MD 20762-7002

SUBJECT: HQ AFOSI Response to Draft Report on the Evaluation of Criminal Investigative
Organizations Policies, Practices, and Procedures for Investigating Child Sexual
Abuse (Project No. 9850011K)

1. I have reviewed the draft report referenced above, and the recommendations as they apply to
AFOSI. Of the six recommendations made in the report, only two are applicable to our
organization. I have attached a summary of the AFOSI response to these recommendations, with
estimated completion dates.

2. The HQ AFOSI POC for this issue is LtCol (Dr) Nancy A. Slicner, Chief, Violent Crimes
Division. She can be reached at DSN 857-0997, or commercial (240) 857-0997.

LEONARD E. PATTERSON
Colonel, USAF
Commander

Attachment: AFOSI Responses to Draft Report Recommendations

RESPONSE TO DRAFT EVALUATION REPORT RECOMMENDATIONS

Recommendation 1: The MCIOs, during appropriate inspection, staff assistance, or oversight visits to field locations, verify that their criminal investigators involved in child sexual abuse investigations are participating in multidisciplinary teams, coordinating overall investigative activities, and sharing information throughout the investigations.

> **Response:** The current Unit Compliance Inspection (UCI) process is already fulfilling this recommendation. As part of the UCI, detachment's closed case files are reviewed for investigative sufficiency and documentation. During the review of any child sexual abuse investigation, inspectors verify that coordination was completed and documented with a Forensic Science Consultant, as well as medical and legal authorities.

Recommendation 2: The USACIDC, through its Sex Crimes and Child Abuse Monitorship Program, give special emphasis to assuring that only agents trained in interviewing children interview child sexual abuse victims.

> **Response:** Not applicable to AFOSI.

Recommendation 3: The U.S. Army Military Police School block of instruction in Child Abuse Prevention and Investigative Techniques course dealing with child interviews include a lesson plan with leaning objectives and instructor guide to assure consistency in instruction and conformance with Army policy.

> **Response:** Not applicable to AFOSI.

Recommendation 4: The NCIS develop coordinated lesson plans with learning objectives and instructor guides to assure consistency in training and conformance with NCIS policy.

> **Response:** Not applicable to AFOSI.

Recommendation 5: The AFOSI written policy and training on the use of anatomically detailed dolls should be consistent.

> **Response:** Concur. AFOSI policy currently does not specifically address the use of anatomically correct dolls. Policy will be reviewed with specific attention to the use of anatomical dolls and recommendations made for change in accordance with current research findings in this area. Estimated Completion Date (ECD): 1 Dec 01.

Recommendation 6: The Under Secretary of Defense (Personnel & Readiness) review current Armed Forces Center for Child Protection resources and determine if they should be enhanced.

> **Response:** Not applicable to AFOSI.

Evaluation Team Members

Deputy Assistant Inspector General for Criminal Investigative Policy and Oversight, Office of the Assistant Inspector General for Investigations, Office of the Inspector General, Department of Defense.

John J. Perryman, Project Manager

Lt. Colonel Brian A. Braden, Evaluator

Love Silverthorn, Investigative Review Specialist

Randy Knight, Criminal Investigator

Craig Rupert, Criminal Investigator

Scott Russell, Criminal Investigator